# ACKNOWLEDGEMENTS

The poem in the epilogue "Constellations of Waking" is reprinted from *This Constellation Is A Name: Collected Poems 1965-2010* (2012) by permission of Nightboat Books.

Portions of this libretto were collaged to form the poem "Letter & Dream of Walter Benjamin" originally published in *This Constellation Is A Name: Collected Poems 1965-2010* (2012) by permission of Nightboat Books.

The photograph accompanying the "Epilogue" on page (109) shows a portion of the glass-fronted base wall of the *Passagen—Hommage à Walter Benjamin* by the Israeli artist Dani Karavan created at Port Bou in 2005. The inscription in German from Benjamin's writing sandblasted on the glass can be translated as: "It is more arduous to honor the memory of the nameless [Namenlosen] than that of the renowned. Historical construction is devoted to the memory of the nameless [Gedächtnis der Namenlosen]."

for Ellen,

and for the performers, musicians and technicians
who brought this work to life

# Author's Note

This work was originally conceived in collaboration with the composer and video artist Ellen Fishman Johnson as the libretto of an opera for voices, instruments, video and phantasmagoria (magic lantern). It premiered in concert version under the title "Benjamin" at the Philadelphia Fringe Festival in 2000. Much of the text is a reworking and re-arranging of material taken from Walter Benjamin's correspondence and writings. The text for pre-recording for Scene III is from Berthold Brecht's poem "The Darkest Times 1940-IV." The poem "Constellations of Waking" in the Epilogue is by the author. See Sources on page 119-120.

# TABLE OF CONTENTS

# PREFACE
(in lieu of overture)

There I was in the nineteen-sixties sitting on an Andalusian beach under the cliffs on which perched the little town of Nerja, Spain. I was just beginning to think of myself as a writer. A little poetry prize the year before, like the shot of a starter's pistol, had propelled me across the Atlantic in search of . . . in search of what I was not quite sure. Best to say, with as little embarrassment as possible, that I was ripe for literature, for poetry, not because I had a career in mind, but because I seemed to be simultaneously finding both words and myself, and that discovery came like a rush, as good a high as I had ever experienced.

Within a few months of arrival, I met the Irish novelist Aidan Higgins, ten years my senior, well-read beyond my NYC-American provincialisms. He gave me books by European writers to read, Musil, Broch, Canetti, bits of Beckett about whom I knew a little (I had seen *Godot*, and read *Murphy, Malone Dies* and *The Unnamable*). But I remember most—in fact I have never forgotten--that day, well before Walter Benjamin's name was circulated in American intellectual circles, when Aidan handed me a copy of his *Illuminations*. It had just been published in the United Kingdom, translated into English by Harry Zohn, and with a complex and powerful biographical introduction by Hannah Arendt that deeply probed Benjamin's thought and wanderings. I am remembering how moved I was, not only by the thought and intellect of the work, but by how Arendt's introduction laid me open to his life in ways that I am still exploring. That paperback copy, heavily underlined and marked up, is still with me, though I have bought a half a dozen other copies as I've moved around in my travels.

Many years later, I read Susan Sontag's 1980 essay on Walter Benjamin, "Under the Sign of Saturn" which beautifully articulates

Benjamin's deep psychic appeal for me. There, she reminds us that Saturn is the planet of wobbles, of an erratic orbit that brings it now nearer, now farther from the sun. "Erratic" and "errancy" have the same root in the archaic meaning of the word "err," *to stray* as well as in its common meaning to make a mistake. It is that erratic motion characterizing Benjamin's life that drew me to him long before I had read Sontag.

In the sixties, I was undergoing my own bout of errancy. Winning that small poetry prize seemed to have sanctioned a break with my then nine-to-five life as a technical writer for a large international corporation, one which led me to cut many ties, pack up my books and decide to spend a year in Spain trying to find myself as a writer. None of it was well-thought out nor even seriously planned, but I was lucky, and after a few months of travel, found myself in Nerja. Not far from the town lay the recently re-discovered and now famous *Cueva de Nerja*, an immense many-chambered subterranean cavern, occupied thousands of years in the past and filled with cave drawings and artifacts.

I'm sure that when Higgins handed me *Illuminations*, my young writer's identification with and hunger for a literary hero was certainly at work, and Benjamin immediately occupied that space in my psyche. As well, my European undertaking was fraught with misgivings and fears that I'd made a horrible blunder of my own. *Errancy, blunders!* In her essay, Arendt describes Benjamin's near-tragic wandering and missteps in both thought and activity as he lived through the flowering and then destruction wrought on the German-Jewish diaspora. She tells of his childhood encounter with "the bungler," a fanciful figure out of German children's tales. Upon some mistake or clumsiness on his part, Benjamin's mother was prone to exclaim "Mr. Bungle sends his regards." My own bungling left me ripe for Benjamin's story. It drew me to him.

I was especially fascinated by his difficulties, by his inability to commit his life wholly to any one of a number of social and political causes, or to settle on any philosophical world-view with certainty. His life was a chronicle of dis-ease and discomfort, a sense, as one studied him, of his never feeling at home. Benjamin's "bungling," his difficulty at all points in his life to comply with the social and professional norms of his milieu seemed to set the psychological and later critical and philosophical pathways of his errancy. Benjamin himself, across the arc of his life, recognized this aspect in himself. In one of his last letters of 1940, the year of his most frightening imperilment and finally suicide, he wrote to Arendt:

> I would be in deeper depression than the one by
> which I am currently gripped if, as bookless as I
> am, I had not found in the only book I do have the
> aphorism that is most splendidly appropriate to my
> current state: "His laziness supported him in glory
> for many years in the obscurity of an errant and
> hidden life" (La Rochefoucauld speaking to Retz)"
> (*WBC* 637)

"Laziness" does not seem an apt description of a life lived so actively and, often, frenetically. But there is a sense of an almost determined kind of "laziness," something resembling a reflective pause, in Benjamin's refusal to be a man of action, to go with conventional expectations. In truth, this cultivated hiatus, this hesitation before the next step into commitment is at the very heart of the romance of Benjamin's complicated life, the poignancy of his wanderings and ultimately the tragic misstep of his suicide. And as I read and increased my knowledge, I was more possessed by these missteps than by any theorizing or philosophical teaching that could be drawn from his writings.

As I saw it, Benjamin's story, though far more heroic in every regard than mine, nevertheless resonated with some of my own experience at the time. I had started writing a few years earlier. Nerja in the 1960s was a place in transition, and so was I. For me, the journey to Nerja had been a nearly inarticulate commitment to writing, to poetry. I had given up job, apartment, seeing good friends, to reorient my life, and in my perfect fantasy, I envisioned the strange, beautiful caves of Nerja as both constant metaphor and reality for the process I was undergoing. To the extent that I was a *spelunker* of its passages, I was also a wanderer of my own inner life. Later, as I came to read more deeply into Benjamin's work, the psychological intertwining and identifications, the blundering, "the errant and hidden life," struck me as the very heart of his empowering empathy, his intellectual stances, his profound understanding of culture, literature and politics. More than with most thinkers I have encountered, Benjamin's life, the difficult and obstruction-ridden life, its unsettled quality, felt inseparable from his writing. My own experiences and this seed-syllable, this romance of Benjamin's dis-ease and uncertainty, was, in retrospect, what would ultimately lead to the libretto/poem of this book.

*

I believe it was this inseparability that led Arendt to write that Benjamin "thought poetically." By this, she was in no way suggesting that Benjamin's style was "poetic" or flowery, rather that in its search for truth, Benjamin's understandings were shaped by the "reality" of his encounters. He was, she wrote, an "alchemist practicing the obscure art of transmuting the futile elements of the real into the shining, enduring gold of truth." Surely it was a negative alchemy he practiced. His rejection of certainties, of comforting ideologies and dogmas, resembles a poetics, in Arendt's words, of "watching and interpreting the historical process," of bringing about a "magical transfiguration" hitherto neither recognized nor even articulated. This "poetics" arose out of a refusal to be grounded in either idealism or the shabby realism of the dark positivist outlook that pervaded the European culture of Benjamin's time.

*

 As I write this, I'm looking at my Schocken copy of *Illuminations* published in the United States in 1969, purchased, as my note on the flyleaf shows, on December 11, 1969, a few years after my return. In the essay "The Image of Proust," Benjamin lays great emphasis on Proust's physical condition, how his asthma "became part of his art." He writes that unlocking Proust requires an understanding of the author's "physiology of style." Everywhere, intellect, psychology and physical being, thoroughly intermixed, make up what we mean by "Proust."

 In 1969, I underlined a passage in this essay that read: "He lay on his bed racked with homesickness, homesick for the world distorted in the state of resemblance, a world in which the true surrealist face breaks through." Here that physiology and bodily state of being in its contingency to the world becomes a kind of knowledge, a politics even, of vision. Though ostensibly about Proust, the passage strikes me as deeply autobiographical. In these words, Benjamin seems to characterize his own adult life, suffused with a feeling of homelessness, of inner and outer exile, not as alienation but as a profound knowledge of the split between the conventions of reality and the truth of "the surrealist face" that undermines the social and political structures offered up by culture.

 "Homesickness." A longing, painful, dispiriting condition. We must understand that Benjamin's homelessness was not the result of a "*Wanderjahr,*" a joyful trek into new lands and unknowns. It always had a melancholic character, a sense of sadness and lostness, painfully sharpened by its unsought contingency to the terrible events of the twentieth century, the World Wars, the Shoah, the personal loss of friends, of career and hope in human possibility. As Arendt explains, we cannot understand Benjamin without understanding the "element of bad luck" which permeated his existence.

*

Benjamin's hero against complacency is Baudelaire, the poet who in much of his writing seeks to render the lives of the poor, the dispossessed and the hoodwinked. "Official" political and social reality is the hoodwinker; it is unexamined, conventional or sophistical in its ability to disguise the ruptures in the social order lying before it. In his series of notes and reflections entitled *Central Park*, Benjamin refers to Baudelaire's "Tableaux parisiens," writing that it exposes the urban landscape, the one most familiar to the poet, as "no longer a homeland." True, this process can be described as a kind of "de-familarization," but it is not a conscious strategy "to make strange" as in surrealism or other experimental modes. As Benjamin sees it in Baudelaire, it is more clearly a response, a "shock defense" as he calls it, where everything is made strange by circumstance, by economic and social forces and by the poet's close attention to details that expose the gaps between official and actual reality.

Benjamin's meditations on Baudelaire and on Poe's "man of the crowd" register the shock of the urban environment. Baudelaire's discomfort at being jostled by the crowd is partly the horror of being carried along by senselessness, by the movement of sluggish mentalities easily diverted by commodity culture and by the allure of the erotics of the urban scene. But in his study of the poet, Benjamin also sees simultaneously a generative act, one producing the intervention that poetry can accomplish. "Every second," he writes," finds consciousness ready to intercept its shock," as though it were the poet's task not only to be on guard for society's outrages but to be able to articulate a response to them that embodies hope. It is a unique dynamic, one that sees the poet less as *enfant terrible* than as spiritual and cultural guide.

What are these dynamics? For Benjamin, literary works were "hieroglyphs of redeemed life," data points or concretions (which, to borrow from the history of our own poetics, resemble somewhat Poundian images or gists and piths), meant to rescue individuals and even whole epochs from the darknesses that recur in chronological time.  The hieroglyph-shock was a kind of dynamic intersection in the arena in which history met the possibilities of knowledge and redemption.  This was his "now-time" (or *jetztzeit*) poetics, his "messianic moment," instances where language and thought come together as both prophecy and dread.  Out of misfortune, which he saw all around him, hope could arise.  He viewed these terms both poetically and politically, as interferences and shocks to the system to be critiqued and pried open to allow freedom, both economic and social, to be engendered.  Even his notion of the photograph as the "posthumous moment," which he linked to the Kabbalistic ideal of *Devekut* or "adhesion" created a point in time where redemption was possible.

*

Re-reading Benjamin forcefully reminds me of how much of his work involves quotation  --and how many of his strategies and techniques, in their wrenching bits of language from their original contexts, resemble the act of quotation (he wanted to write a book that was all quotation, and almost succeeded with his *Arcades* project).  In a world in which authoritarian and fascist totalization of a society had undermined and transformed historical memory, Benjamin believed that the only way to bring forward a useable vision of an unfalsified past was through citation, citation which would, of its nature, induce "shock" to the powers that be.  As he famously put it: "quotations in my works are like robbers by the roadside who make an armed attack and relieve an idler of his convictions" (*I* 38).  Benjamin's use of citation, as Arendt observed, was destructive, aimed at breaching the walls of the "professional preservers" who manned the ramparts of the fascist state.

This use of citations, as well as the rearrangements of fragments of letters, instantaneous observations and contingent felicities of phrasing inspired my construction of this work.  Every bit of data held, as Benjamin had said of each day of the calendar, the messianic possibility of redemption.

*

The aspects of his life-story that make it an "opera," a drama, a novel (of which there have been many) consist of his intellectual and emotional "poetics," the joy of knowledge and discovery which in its way is also an armory of stances and techniques, of survival strategies governed by his ethics—all of this set against a time of catastrophe and ruin.   It was this kind of truth-seeking that for me ultimately transforms the romance of his life into an exemplum, with a use-value for those who read and try to understand his work.

Those poetics also governed me as I wrote the original libretto for *Constellations of Waking*.  I wanted to express Benjamin's "home-lessness," both physical and emotional, in terms of his conception of shock--shock as a poetic principle (as he had derived it from Henri Bergson and Freud), something he found in his reading of Baude-laire.

What brought the messianic elements together into a coher-ent, useable linguistic structure was montage, which could bring over into historical analysis, as Benjamin wrote, "the crystal of the total event in the analysis of the simple individual moment."  Mon-tage sunders the purposeful chains of chronicle, those stories which mandate "official" sense and "official" views.  Chronicle and official history were to be broken open to reveal their contradictions and ambiguities so that another logic could be impelled, one contrary to the flow of time which had the revolutionary power to build into the views of culture a new structure of relations that I have called else-where "counter-continuities."**

If there were any hope for political or cultural redemption, it would arise from such a "now-time" poetics, a messianic shock which fused knowledge of the past with an open-ended critique of the pres-ent.  For Benjamin, this could only be supplied by art or "historical materialism," which as he defines it, lies closer to poetry than history.

*

Benjamin continues in my life as both example and resource. In the mid-nineties, after many collaborations with the Philadelphia composer, Ellen Fishman Johnson, we decided to embark on an opera about him. The catalyst was the availability of the large selection of his correspondence, translated into English, published by the University of Chicago Press in 1994. By 1996, Harvard was undertaking the publication in English of nearly all his writings, including the Arcades Project, a six volume endeavor with more to come. These resources gave me fuller access not only to Benjamin's thought but also to the day to day life he led. For me, the letters brought more of Benjamin the person into focus, his hopes, failures, self-critiques and assessments of what he read, views of his friends and those he disagreed with, his daily hopes and struggles. Given the immense hoard of Benjamin materials now translated and the many memoirs and writings about him, it seemed impossible to create any work that could be considered comprehensive. Instead, the composer and I undertook to follow out a project based on Benjamin's own conceptions of creation. Thus "Constellations of Waking" is an attempt to render specific moments in Benjamin's life, yet suggest the flavor of the totality that made up his existence. The form, which is closer to oratorio than opera, tries to convey the richness of Benjamin's life in crystalline form.

According to recent star maps, the planet Saturn in its wobbling transit moves through such well-known constellations as Scorpio and Sagittarius, momentarily altering their configurations. Like those star-clusters in the night sky, this work is made up of data points and imaginary containment lines, now-times and prophetic moments. I hope that something of the passage of the earthly cosmos that was Walter Benjamin is figured in it.

*from *A Berlin Chronicle*, 1932, published in 1970.
** see my "Avant-Garde Propellants of the Machine Made of Words" in *Uncertain Poetries: Essays on Poets, Poetry and Poetics* by Michael Heller (Shearsman Books, 2012).

# CHARACTERS
(in order of appearance)

CHORUS, mixed voices also functioning as
NARRATORS, YOUNG PEOPLE and EXTRAS.

BELMORE, Benjamin's friend in youth in Berlin

WALTER BENJAMIN, writer and critic.

HEINLE (and HEINLE'S GHOST), Young idealistic poet and Benjamin's
    close friend.

CARLA, Benjamin's intimate friend and correspondent in youth.

GERHARD SCHOLEM, (Gershom Sholem) historian, thinker, Benjamin's
    life-long friend.

ASJA LACIS, Benjamin's lover and occasional collaborator.

REICH, Asja's lover and Soviet party functionary.

MEYERHOLD, experimental theater director, shot during Stalin's purges.

DORA, Benjamin's divorced wife.

BERTHOLD BRECHT, poet, playwright and drama theoretician.

ADORNO, the thinker.

SAHL, writer and philosopher, companion with Benjamin in the
    concentration camp at Nevers.

# SYNOPSIS

## Prologue:  All Decisive Blows

For Benjamin, as his friend Ernst Bloch put it, the future was "unfated," hence all blows, all experiences were to be seen as coming from unexpected quarters, in his case, the "left hand" of unknowing and surprise.  Benjamin's "now-time" poetics, messianic arrest and shock do not so much constitute a thought-out strategy for dealing with uncertainty or violent contingencies as suggest a posture or way of being in the world that seeks to be responsive to what might happen next.  The voice in the left hand column reworks Benjamin's words on contingency.  The video voices come from passages in the writings of Leslie Fisko, Benjamin's companion on the arduous hike in the Pyrennes to the Spanish border station as the party attempted to flee Nazi occupied France, recalling the event that ultimately led to Benjamin's death, the refusal to be granted entry into Spain, after which Benjamin returned to his hotel in Port Bou and committed suicide.  In this sense, the prologue's two intertwining choral voices make for an arc leaping from Benjamin's critical thought to the final events of his life.

## Scene I.  Berlin 1914:  Language of Youth and the Death of Fathers

By 1914, all of Europe anticipates war.  Benjamin is 22, still a student and a member of the pacifist-leaning Youth Movement.  He converses with Herbert Belmore, a close boyhood friend and school mate, also a member of the movement.  From the beginning of his student days, Benjamin has sought to grapple with difficult literary and philosophical subjects.  His dialogues with Belmore concern the falsity of a conservative adult viewpoint that belittles the idealism of youth.  One of Benjamin's earliest essays, "Experience," written in 1913, begins: "In our struggle for responsibility, we fight against someone who is masked. The mask of the adult is called 'experience.'" The essay attacks "mature" rationalizations and temporizing; it counsels the negation of the prohibitions parents impose on their sons and daughters. Benjamin and Belmore argue and discuss, but such dialogues between young people in different stages of consciousness and sophistication are really clashes between psychic and historical eras. Unlike their elders, the young refuse to accept the dictates of "experience." But then, the most horrible of experiences—real war—intrudes, and some members of the Youth Movement, in their disillusionment, commit suicide, among these Frederich Heinle, the young idealistic poet, one of Benjamin's closest friends.

### Intermezzo: Gerhard and Walter Play Thinker's Chess

In which the rhetorical battle between idealism and bourgeois life becomes a matter of mate and checkmate, of language and silence.

### Scene II. Moscow 1926: Moscow Diary

Benjamin seeks to re-ignite his romance with his former lover Asja Lacis and to confirm his feelings about Marxism and the Russian Revolution. He travels to Moscow in the depths of winter. His inability to read or speak Russian leaves him isolated and dependent on others to gain any insight into the cultural and social transformations taking place before his eyes. Disappointments follow. Asja has a new lover Reich, and remains throughout Benjamin's visit extremely standoffish. And Benjamin, slowly becomes disillusioned with Russian life under Stalin's transformations. He observes in the situation of the director Meyerhold (later murdered in one of Stalin's purges) the dangerous fierceness of culture critique. About his Moscow experiences, he writes back to Berlin: "the tensions of public life—which in a large part have an almost theological character—are so great that, to an unimaginable degree, they seal off everything private."

## Intermezzo: A New Game Of Chess

An imaginary game of geographies, where to live, where to think and be?  Benjamin had a number of opportunities to both visit and to emigrate to Palestine where a strong Jewish social and intellectual culture existed, one which so captured Scholem's affections that by 1925 he had moved permanently to Jerusalem.  Benjamin, although obsessed with Judaic culture, maintained his "faith" in Europe until the last few months of his life.

## Scene III. Svendborg 1934: The Brecht Time

Benjamin's friendship and connection with Brecht dates from 1929.  Brecht seems to have mesmerized Benjamin, and as one biographer puts it, "His relationship to Brecht is in fact, qualitatively different from that with any other of his contemporaries: it is characterized  by a certain awe and even subservience that is nowhere else evident" (WB 452).  By the time Benjamin visits Brecht in Svendborg, Hitler has become Chancellor of Germany, and the social order is now in the hands of a raving, anti-Semitic authoritarian.  The fate of the proletariat, the economic and cultural order of society are in doubt, topics Benjamin and Brecht have discussed since they first met in the nineteen twenties.  But in Svendborg, Benjamin, penniless and visiting Brecht partly because he can afford no place else to live, seems unduly under Brecht's influence, an influence that many of Benjamin's friends and colleagues do not consider healthy.

**Intermezzo: Letter Exchange**

Benjamin and Scholem correspond. The Nazi totalitarian state encircles a despairing Benjamin, his few pleasures reduced to his library and to the research he is doing. The two friends call across time and space to each other, Benjamin's voice in anguish, Scholem's in a prophetic *diktat*.

**Scene IV. Paris 1939: In the Arcades**

Paris was for Benjamin the scene of his most powerful experiences. After his first visit in 1913, he wrote: "instead of having a few memories of this city I could tell you about, I have only an awareness of having lived intensely for fourteen days as only children do." His emotions range from extraordinary delight, critical and aesthetic enthusiasm to deep depression and finally despair. His "Arcades" project, inspired by the commercial passageways in the center of Paris are the focus of his most intense researches. "The arcades and interiors," he writes, "the exhibitions and panoramas are residues of a dream world . . . . Each epoch not only dreams the next but also, in dreaming, strives toward the moment of waking." Benjamin's search is for that moment, even as he explores the underlife of Paris, its brothels, casinos and cafes. He meets other European intellectuals, many who have fled the Nazis to find haven here. The great storehouse of the Bibliothèque Nationale becomes his second home. Paris, too, is where Benjamin finally confronts in its full grimace, his impoverished circumstances and the deadly stranglehold of the Nazi Occupation. Much of his time is then spent in correspondence with friends and colleagues, seeking financial aid and assistance to escape the nightmare that Paris has become for him.

**Intermezzo:  Voices In Near Darkness**

At this stage, both Benjamin and Scholem have retreated into
near purity of thought, as though its idealizations were more tangible
than personal circumstance.  Scholem can still argue half-heartedly
with his imperiled friend; Benjamin clings to his ideas as a mountain-
eer clings to his guide rope.

**Scene V.  Paris, Stade Columbe, Nevers 1939-1940:  Internment
and Non-internment**

On September 9th, 1939, Benjamin answers the general edict
of the Occupation officials calling for the interment of foreign Ger-
man and Austrian nationals.  They are commanded to report to the
Stade Columbe, a sports arena on the outskirts of Paris.  Held in the
open stands only partially sheltered from the weather, the internees
are subjected to the elements, to inadequate food and lack of sani-
tary conditions.  Benjamin, already in ill-health, barely survives the
ordeal.  Next come train transport and a forced march to the intern-
ment camp at Nevers.  There, despite ill-health and inadequacies of
both food and medical care, Benjamin, exercises, as his fellow internee
Hans Sahl writes, his "admirable impracticality," offering courses on
literature and philosophy to other inmates of the camp.  Through
the intercession of writers and intellectuals, Benjamin is liberated
from the camp on November 25th and returns to Paris, seeing old
comrades and literary friends.  In November of the following year,
unable to obtain either an exit visa or financial aid, Benjamin flees
with a small group of other endangered foreigners toward the Spanish
border, hoping to cross illegally into the safety of Spain.

**Epilogue: Constellations of Waking**

Two poems: one an elegy for Benjamin who has died by his own hand at Port Bou after being refused entry into Spain; the other constructed from one of Benjamin's dream-letters. It seems to be about the dangers of truly original thinking, the only kind Benjamin was capable of.

# SETTING

The stage area slopes up toward the back and is bisected by a low stepped wall which runs at an angle from the front to back of stage (see artist's design below).  Voices in the lefthand column of the text originate from the stage, though some voices may emanate in the darkness or shadows of the set.  Voices in the righthand column are offstage or via video and sound tracks.  TV monitors and projectors are used to accommodate pre-recorded video and audio portions of the score.  Video projection is across screens on the back wall of the stage, enabling discrete, overlapping or stage-unifying visuals.  Supertitles are displayed on the screens at the beginning of each scene, as are the introductory texts spoken by the Narrators (these should appear word-by-word as they are spoken, slowly filling the screen with the text).  The phantasmagoria (magic lantern) periodically plays over the whole stage, varying its direction.

All staging and stage directions such as left and right are from the audience's perspective and all are provisional and meant as suggestions for a production.

Artist's conception of the set by Bradford Graves

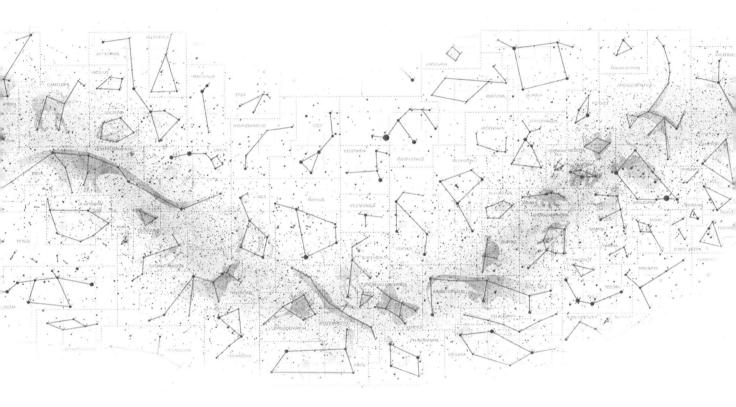

# CONSTELLATIONS
# OF WAKING

# Prologue: All Decisive Blows

| ON STAGE | PRE-RECORDED IMAGES & TEXT FOR MUSIC AND VIDEO |
|---|---|
| *(Empty stage, chorus unseen.)* | |
| CHORUS | |
| All decisive blows are delivered with the left hand. | |
| | **We were unfamiliar with the road** |
| | **Some of it we had to crawl on all fours** |

All decisive blows—
not of one's choosing.

All blows are decisive
when delivered with the left hand.

One is struck,
delivered of a decisive blow,

On judgment day all blows
are delivered with the left hand.

Don't choose. You could not choose.

You did not choose to have blows delivered.


Decisive blows were delivered
to you with the left hand.

**We were unfamiliar
with the road**

**Some of it we had to crawl on all fours**

(*VIDEO screen goes dark.*)

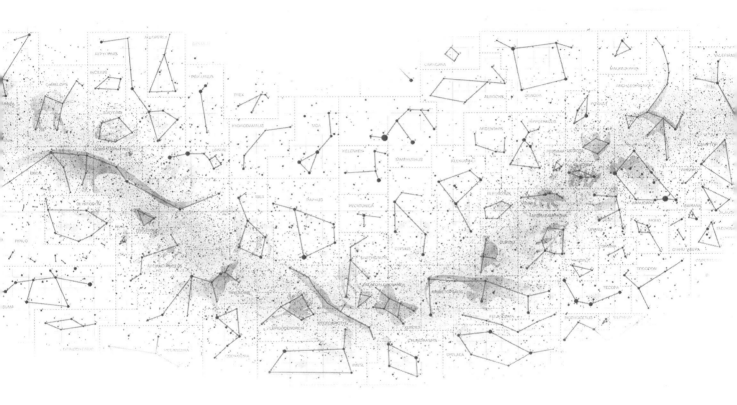

# SCENE I

## Berlin 1914:
## Language of Youth and the Death of Fathers

NARRATORS: *The young students, children of the bourgeois, speak meaningfully but in clichés. They talk about passion, threats of war, oppression. They simplify their language to make it immediate and forceful. Their bodies, their urges, their sexual drives. Their heightened emotions, their need to display intellect and yet be "of the people" in an imitative way. These feelings propel their words. They seek direct lines of force. Nuance is for the corrupt or for the apologists of the status quo, for their gilded fathers and acquiescent mothers. They have only hatred for their professors and for the sophists who applaud themselves with their embroidered rhetorics. Thus two naïvetés co-exist, two self-victimizations: the clear-sightedness of youth; the amused contempt of the academics for direct speech.*

| ON STAGE | PRE-RECORDED IMAGES & TEXT FOR MUSIC AND VIDEO |
|---|---|

*(Benjamin on left side of wall; Belmore on the right.)*

BELMORE

Ah, the Engadine,
the thrall
of its shadowed valley,
and the Jungfrau,
that eternal glacier!

Those pines
you wrote home about,
their soft whispers you say
you heard in the wind.

All Europe, a mythos you now tell us—
you were speaking of a delusion,
of a peace where all
your much loved gods were home.

BENJAMIN

My bookish gods, Isis, page 32
in Wölfflin's *Klassische Kunst*,

Demeter, ibid. page 48, and Pythia,
op. cit.  Op. cit. Pythia!

*(VIDEO: Berlin 1914.  Youth movements. Literature, Art, Politics.  Memories of vacations, the Alps, Italy.  War just over the horizon.)*

*(Youthful voices.)*

**"Brother now may we
your companions be
in the world so wide"**

**What we want**

**What we want**

8

The goddess speaks ambiguously,
in a voice no longer fully heard,
in a voice that barely utters words.

More the sound
of a clock between ticks,
edgy, liminal, uncertain of form.

Not a silky voice between pines
but a suppressed babble.

Why won't she say more to me?

BELMORE

The young man romancing the unknowable!
You'll quote Hölderlin next.

Dear Walter, lift your head from the page.

There's a slump in your back.
O frail youth, at times you resemble
those old Jews davening in shul.

Your eyes shred text,
your mouth emits nonsense.

Consult something real!

**Will it take anything
from a young person?**

**What we want
from a new
youthfulness—**

**will it make us
less lonely?**

BENJAMIN

I partake of their mumbling, my
mumbling.

Pythia thinks the matter
that makes up this world
weighs almost nothing,
that our heavy spirits
outweigh it far too much,

that the world's matter overburdens us.

BELMORE

Walter, you make riddles out of words.
You are a sphinx.

BENJAMIN
(*As though to himself.*)

O Pythia, who can understand our Pythia?
Like all oracles, when she speaks
it is someone else's words.

I am the suppliant, and note her foretellings.
I drink the dregs from Lethe's cup.

Our European life, it weighs too much,
it weighs too much.

(*Single voice.*)

**I tried to summon up,
in a meditation
on lyric poetry,
the figure
of my friends**

BELMORE
(*sarcastically*)

O weighty matter! O politics!
Has your fortuneteller
brought you up to date?

War is approaching—

and besides,
wouldn't you like to pitch
into the waters of the Spree,
the Kaiser's sabre rattling in its sheath,
toss in as well those little brats,
the tin soldiers marching
before the Brandenburg gate.

Tell me you hear the sounds:
the caterpillars munching linden leaves
on Unter den Linden,
and politicians working up steam,
blaming the caterpillars on Jews
and Bolsheviks.

BENJAMIN

Our youth no longer youth.

I'm bitten clean from old romantic lies.

**I tried to summon up
the figure
of my friends**

**The image is now
that of a dead man**

BELMORE

My, you are in a state.

BENJAMIN

Yes, the state of Germany!

BELMORE and BENJAMIN

And so much weighty matter
leaves no room, leaves no place
for a pretty goddess to sit,

for a pretty goddess to take her seat,
op. cit., op. cit., even
in a railway car in transit
across all Europe
from Siracusa to Archangel.

(*Pause.*)

BELMORE

Is our hero still depressed?

BENJAMIN

Our hero is still depressed.

(*All voices.*)

**Who to appease
the clamorous shades
of the dispossessed
by philanthropic
ceremonies?**

BELMORE

We *Wandervögel*, tripping
over ourselves.

BENJAMIN

Where are those who are solitary, today?

BELMORE

Walking birds
—awaken our youth.

BENJAMIN

Explode the logic of the fathers!

Today, I have a premonition
slogans won't do.

Instead, let's compose a novella
and entitle it *Death of the Father*.

BELMORE

The *death* of the father?
I *wonder* what that will be about?

BENJAMIN

Europe as dying father.

BELMORE

Oh yes, I know,
the generations who botched it.

So far, I'm unimpressed with the idea.

But what next?

BENJAMIN

I'll tell my story
in literary symbols.

BELMORE

Are you sure
the bourgeoisie can follow?

BENJAMIN

The true task of language is the crystal-clear
elimination of the unsayable.

*Listen*, a father dies.

BELMORE

I've got *that* idea!

BENJAMIN

*Good!*

Shortly after,
on the very same day
of his father's death,
the son seduces
the young maid of the house.

Nine months later,
this maid has a child.

BELMORE

Yes, yes,
I get that idea too.

—and then?

BENJAMIN

The maid insists
on giving the child
the dead father's name.

BELMORE

Hmmmmm . . .

(*Duo:*)

**You will find us
lying together
in the meeting house.**


**You will find us
lying together,
hand in hand,
in the meeting house.**

BENJAMIN

Call it Europe.

BELMORE

Wait!  Call whom Europe?

BENJAMIN

You see, it is all new,
something only the young
could have created.

BELMORE

I suppose the father
ruled the boy's life,
dictating what to read
and what to think?

BENJAMIN

And the maid,

the maid had no
learning to speak of . . .

The word Europe
was meaningless to her.

BENJAMIN and BELMORE

(*In lewd collusion.*)

But she ruled the boy
with her body!

BENJAMIN

I'd let it happen to me!

BELMORE

Delicious, but aren't
you being a little too dumb?

BENJAMIN

I'd let it happen to me.

BELMORE

Oh!  Triumph of feeling over intellect?

A Movement idea.

Walter, you're too smart to believe in that.

BENJAMIN

A story of a time to come,
when the old rules are over.

When we redeem the unredeemable.

BELMORE

Sounds like a cliché to me.
Can we just go back to being funny?

BENJAMIN

When we explode the logic of the fathers.

(*Heinle enters, walking quickly.*)

HEINLE

Have you seen Rika?

BENJAMIN

No, I haven't seen her, but stop a moment.
Your face is pale, as though the universe
were scrubbed from it.

HEINLE

The news is bad.

I'm going to the meeting house.

BENJAMIN

What news, why are you running

HEINLE

I must find Rika.

Did you get my letter?
I sent it last night,
Express.

BENJAMIN
(*Touches his jacket.*)

I have it here.
Tonight I will read it.

HEINLE

Good.

(*Heinle runs off stage.*)

BELMORE

He is in a state.

(*Blackout. Pause.*)

(*Suddenly, war sounds in the music. Stage in semi-darkness. Young people march over the*

*stage, slam into the wall, bang on it with their
hands and heads, fall to the ground. BENJA-
MIN and BELMORE wander through stage
left examining the fallen bodies, turning them
this way and that in order to identify them.
CARLA enters, examining the fallen bodies as
BENJAMIN is doing.)*

CARLA

Have you seen my sister?

BENJAMIN
(*Points to the ground.*)

Here is Rika.
Have you seen Heinle, my friend?

CARLA
(*Points to the ground.*)

Here he is, beside Rika.
They are holding hands.

Among the dead,
my sister and her lover.

BELMORE

The two swore
a pact, to end their lives
if war came.

**Who to appease . . .**


**Came then, the final
heroic attempt
to change
the attitudes of people
without changing
their circumstance**

**their circumstance**


**LANGUAGE OF YOUTH
LANGUAGE OF YOUTH**


**LANGUAGE OF YOUTH**

20

BENJAMIN

So many dead,
her sister and my friend.

CARLA

Was your friend among the dead?

BENJAMIN

Was it your sister who loved my friend?

(*Slowly stage begins to lighten.
BENJAMIN and CARLA can see each other.
BELMORE exits.*)

CARLA

Tell me what you remember.

BENJAMIN

Of the time before the war?

The rooms we rarely left?

A window, the one you heard about,
overlooking a poplar tree,
that shaded children who play.

(*Video and sound stop*)

CARLA

We will miss being alone.

BENJAMIN

We will miss being alone.

Will we feel at home thinking of childhood
under a poplar tree which shades children
at play?

CARLA

We will miss being alone.

CARLA and BENJAMIN

We were beginning to feel at home
in our childhood which the present
wants us to forget.

We will miss being alone.

(*Benjamin takes Heinle's letter from his jacket
and begins to read aloud.*)

"You will find us
lying together
in the meeting house..."

(*Stage lights dim.*)


(HEINLE'S GHOST *enters.*)


HEINLE (*as ghost*)

Too young to walk ramparts,
father of nothing
and nothingness,

saw Europe die,
took my life
to endstop this nothingness.

Walter believed
what I could not.
He was never
engulfed in nothingness.

He and Gerhard
made their Kafka holy,
pored over their meretricious
kabbalah to dispel doubt.

Torah, law,
Book-crammed shelves.

O language: spectacular
in its failure.  Why discuss

the betterment of
this impoverished progress?

Walter wrote,
'the most genuine
feeling for nature
is dread.'

World, human—
its armies roll across
a countryside, a border—

human nature?
"travel defenseless"
said my Hölderlin.

No need to be a nihilist,
I think life looked
unworthy from there.

Ridiculous!

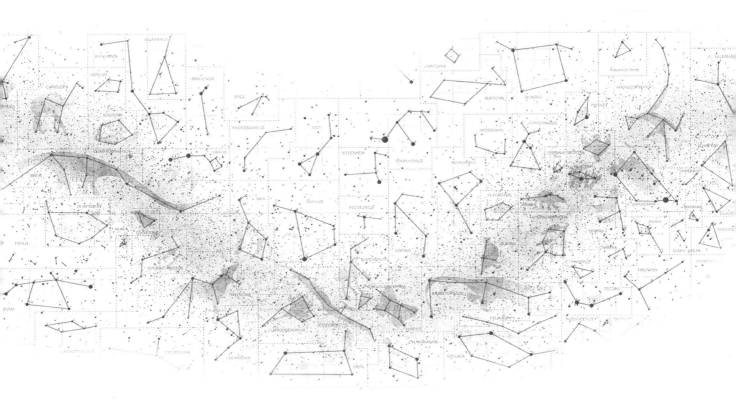

♟♟♟♟♟♞♝♚♛♚♝♞♟♟♟♟

## Intermezzo: Gerhard and Walter Play Thinker's Chess

<table>
<tr><td>ON STAGE</td><td>PRE-RECORDED IMAGES &<br>TEXT FOR MUSIC AND VIDEO</td></tr>
</table>

*(A chessboard is on the dividing wall and BENJAMIN and SCHOLEM are sitting on either side of the wall, playing chess.)*

BENJAMIN

A week ago I began a letter
to you that ended up
eighteen pages long

I was thinking of
our politicians,
those hastily
put-up men
who garner the laurels
of this small state.

*(SCHOLEM'S voice, loud and authoritative.)*

**Walter harbored
very great expectations
for my understanding
of his world.**

**Walter and Dora, his wife,
were elegantly dressed,
bowing like penguins
in all directions.**

**Such preening
before the haute bourgeoisie
struck me as the height
of bad taste.**

These people
outlive
their brief
immortality

but they leave us
a grubby ration
of murderous hopes
called a nation-state.

No more of these hopes!


SCHOLEM

What then?

BENJAMIN

Thus, I tell you,
a week ago,
I began
this letter.

But it was not possible
for me to go
into mathematics and language,
into mathematics and thought,
into mathematics and Zion

**At the same time,
Walter was deeply
offended
by what he called
my "outrageous
wholesomeness."**

It is not possible
for me to go
into Zion.

SCHOLEM
(*To himself.*)

And I can't talk of Zion
with the Zionists!

BENJAMIN

Gerhard, our path
is with the word;
let us prepare
the purest and holiest
places for it.

SCHOLEM

*Impossible.*

BENJAMIN

After the Fall,
the bliss of mute nature
is sadness.

The black letters
of the Written Law
specify the whiteness
between the letters.

Under the word,
the paradise of muteness

or God's unknowable name.

SCHOLEM

Are we speaking
of your lost friends,
of the war which took them?

BENJAMIN

Of war?

Only of the purest
and most holy.

SCHOLEM

Only of the most mute.

**Impossible.**

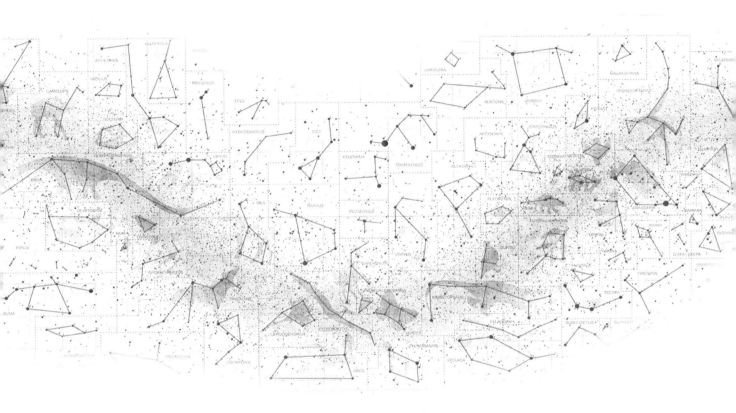

## SCENE II

### Moscow 1926: Moscow Diary

NARRATORS: *The language of totality—breached only by disruptive accounts of feelings, erotics, despair or even the communal care of one for another, for others, that still reside in solitudes and ironies. Privacy, the linguistic self, sheltered hotel rooms in the warrens of the State panopticon, are treasonous. To speak publicly without risking arrest requires tangents, sidereal diagramless elements of language that may mystify the authorities but preserve self-ownership of the psyche even as one's body has become the down payment for "comradeship."*

| ON STAGE | PRE-RECORDED IMAGES & TEXT FOR MUSIC AND VIDEO |
|---|---|

*(Upper right is Benjamin's hotel room in Moscow. Upper left is Asja's room in the sanatorium. Benjamin lies, fully dressed, on the bed. Asja, wearing a hospital smock, lies on her bed.)*

*(VIDEO: Moscow 1926. Winter. Snow drifts. Crowded trams and theaters. Lenin's icon in store windows. Peasants from the villages selling wooden toys on the streets.)*

BENJAMIN

These petit bourgeois
interiors—

the battlefields
over which the assault
has swept.

How to make even
this ice-locked city
a paradise?

By order of the proletariat,
my heart aches unlawfully,
but it aches.

Politics
and love clash

like planets thrown
from orbits.

*(Solo voice.)*

**If we think of it,
we'll wake you.**

**But if we don't
think of it,
we won't.**

**Actually, we usually
think of it,
in which case,
we do wake you up.**

**But to be sure,
we also occasionally
forget to
when we don't
think of it.**

**In which case,
we don't!**

ASJA

I am blunted
by anxieties.

BENJAMIN

Nothing human
can thrive here,

not the Revolution,
not my love,
not myself.

It seems only the toys
the peasants sell
on the street
are granted safe asylum.

ASJA

I am blunted
by anxieties.

BENJAMIN

I think of her,
I want her.

I read Proust in my room
while eating marzipan.

ASJA

I feel uneasy in his presence.

One hour I'm impelled
to address him
by the formal Sie.

At other times,
his presence commands
the informal Du.

BENJAMIN

Twice she called to me,
Du, Du!
Twice she thrilled
by a single word.

Twice my heart
fluttered,
a grosbeak
lost in Moscow's snows.

Twice
thought gave wing
to summers ago
on Capri.

What cold outside.
My hair is very electric here.

ASJA

Yesterday,
as he was leaving,
I ran my fingers
through his hair.

Old days come back.
We were visitors
at Capri
bathing in the sea.

Love talk,
chatter about oppression,
sweetness and politics.

What heady foam
like spindrift
on a thunderous wave.

We mingled unawares in heat.

Now Moscow shuts us in,
alive to everything
important
but blackening
with frost
the petty shoots of love.

BENJAMIN

So cold, my hair

is very electric here,
and the streets
are sheets of ice.

One walks in zigzags
with flailing arms.

ASJA

I bought galoshes
for his feet
and Reich complained.
I was Walter's lover on Capri.

BENJAMIN

She was my lover on Capri.
What sun, what touching
golden days.

In Moscow, she buys
galoshes for my feet.

One walks in zigzags
on these streets.

ASJA

He eats marzipan in his room
and translates Proust,
and Reich complains.

## BENJAMIN

Her new lover Reich—
a decent chap—
all party and the like!

One walks in zigzags
on these streets.

## ASJA

He eats marzipan in his room.

## BENJAMIN

So cold—
sidewalks, bleak, unpaved,
hard with frost and ice;
the peasants shiver
in their stalls,
the colors of their toys,
so bright
they glow, a false fire.

False fire,
our feelings strained.

One walks in zigzags
on these streets.

(*Wall comes down, flush with floorboards. Interior of The Meyerhold Theater. The performance of The Government Inspector has just ended. To one side, a large absurdly drawn map showing Russia massively out of proportion with the rest of Europe. Chorus seated in chairs facing forward. In front of chorus, Benjamin to the right, Reich in the center, Asja at the left. All three seated on chairs facing forward. Applause, and Meyerhold comes from the left to the center of the stage, faces chorus, bows and turns to face audience.*)

MEYERHOLD

Yes, tell me what you think!
The people must have images
of themselves given in
even the most alien work.

REICH

Why silk and velveteen
for fourteen costume gowns
when peasants starve
right on our streets?

MEYERHOLD

Put kulaks and reactionaries
on stage in serf's rags?

(*Video of crowded sumptuously decorated stage.*)

CHORUS

**Hundreds of wax candles
in chandeliers
hanging from above.**

40

Let the Party strip brocade
from those who actually wear it.

My actors know such finery
is shameful to the eyes
of the proletariat.

But I must depict!

I must fill the stage
with such an atmosphere
that action can only
be understood through
a prismatic cloud
that states the Party's case.

REICH

Our proletariat
is still too weak.
It will succumb
to envy.

MEYERHOLD

I want to give them strength!

See how, on stage,
I used your official map
of Europe
where other states
are but a few small

**Little black Uzbecki dwarfs**
**filling the stage**
**with stupefying perfumes,**
**dropping the attar**
**from cut-glass flasks**
**onto platinum**
**heated to a white**
**hot heat.**

**Little blackened men,**
**like the mysterious forces**
**of the oppressed,**
**flitting on stage**
**to pluck fallen**
**lace handkerchiefs**
**from off the floor.**

**Little soiled ones,**
**wretched of the earth**
**pushing chairs under**
**the tired actors,**

strips of land
sticking out from
our vast soviets?

REICH

Our surveyors have been true
to the people.

MEYERHOLD

So has their contempt
for the people's intelligence.

REICH

*Careful!*
Materialist geography
has its use,
but the people's miserable envy
must still be replaced.

MEYERHOLD

So must this bloated
State geography!

(*Meyerhold and Reich begin tugging in
opposite directions at the map, yelling at each
other.*)

**holding their swords,**
**haunting the stage**
**in semi-darknesses.**

**Little ones,**
**clearing away**
**the furniture**
**of the stage.**

**Little ones**
**whose presences**
**make for dark light**
**illuminating the stage.**

MEYERHOLD and REICH

Let go, let go,
let go, let go.

(*Reich succeeds in wrestling away the map,
puts it on his chair and sits on it.*)

BENJAMIN

How quietly the people watch,
each one wordless,
each one a mass verdict.

MEYERHOLD

I sought to give
them strength.

See here, my notes
(*He reads from a sheet of paper.*)

"The longing for life.
The summons to work.
Tragic feeling against a
(background of) comedy.

Happiness—it is the lot
of the future.  For now
work and loneliness."

BENJAMIN

(*Turns to Asja, and as though completing
Meyerhold's thought.*)

And companionship.  Tonight,
you are beautiful.

ASJA

*I am a worker!*

BENJAMIN

In this frozen machine, still
I seek to be near you.

REICH

Your wife wore all the gowns,
held the most inflated roles.

The people were upset.
They starve, freezing
in our streets.

BENJAMIN

How quietly the people watch,
each one wordless,
each one part of a mass verdict.

MEYERHOLD

My audience must be educated
to be astonished
at the circumstances
under which they function.

REICH

Why this capitalist strumpetry?

MEYERHOLD

Have you seen my records?
(*Begins pulling papers from the files and scat-*
*tering them in the air.*)
"Accounts of the Staff.
Accounts of What People Said
at Intermissions.
Accounts of the Reactions of the Audience.
Accounts of the Stage Hands' Work."

Have you seen these?
Don't you know why decadence
must glitter and delight?

You are a fool.

BENJAMIN

The audience was rapt,
each actor made a gesture,

turned their feelings
into lessons.

MEYERHOLD

The audience was rapt,
let them send me to Siberia.
The audience was rapt.

BENJAMIN

O Asja, turn to me,
even if only like an actor with a gesture.

Now Moscow seems one
agit-prop Guignol.

MEYERHOLD

I produced *The Machine Wreckers* and staged
productions of *Masses Are The Man*. I am a
revolutionary!

ASJA

*I am a worker!*
Nothing that I want is mine.

BENJAMIN

These streets.

Such ice which masters a man
by making him relearn
to walk.

The child masters the toy
by holding it in his hand.

MEYERHOLD

The audience holds
the actor and the scene
in its hands.

The audience relearns
to walk.

REICH

The audience is our teacher!

BENJAMIN

The ice masters the audience.

(*Stage goes dark. Stage lights come up. We are
back in Benjamin's hotel room. Benjamin and
Asja sit on the bed.*)

BENJAMIN

Is it true, sunflower
seeds may no longer be

chewed in public?

ASJA

Don't you remember
you first met me
while I was buying
almonds in Munich?

BENJAMIN

I can't forget.

For hours I searched
the empty streets,
streets aflame for me,
darting from
the streetcars
and the house gates!

I had to be first
to see you.

(*Benjamin reaches to embrace Asja.*)

ASJA

Be careful, Reich will come.

BENJAMIN

And what?

*(Stage goes dark, then lights come up. Benjamin is seated alone on stage by the wall. He is playing with Russian toys on the flat top surface of the wall.)*

BENJAMIN

We were very close
that evening.
She couldn't make up
her mind to leave.

Finally, she went from my room.
But my evening was full.

As I hold this toy,
I held her.
As I hold this toy,
she was mine.

As I hold this toy,
I savor my love for her.

Tomorrow I leave.

The triumphant progress
of technology
sweeps across the steppes.

We are its toys.

Everything technical
is sacred here.

It would be considered
counterrevolutionary
to think in terms
of tragic love.

Everything technical
is sacred here.

One walks the streets
like a mechanical man.

The ice makes our
passage strange.


(*Stage goes dark.*)

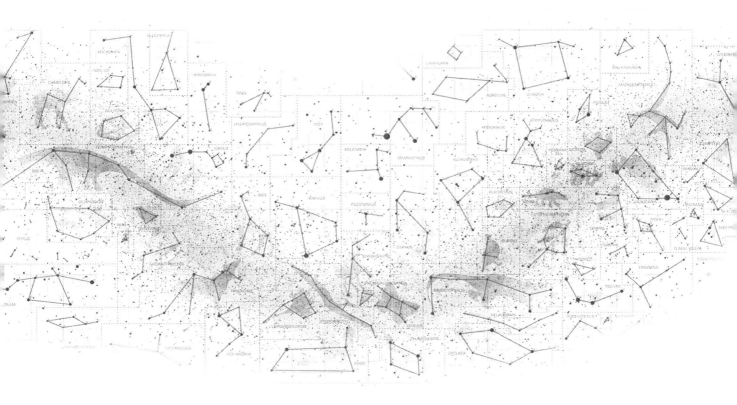

# ♟♟♟♟♟♜♞♝♚♛♝♞♜♟♟♟♟

## Intermezzo: A New Game Of Chess

ON STAGE

*(Benjamin and Scholem play chess. On the screen, the grids of a chessboard are superimposed over a map showing Europe and the Middle East. While the sound track of Scholem's voice plays, the two play chess fiercely, their arms entangled as they try to set pieces down. The moves are displayed on the screen, sometimes two pieces occupying the same square with a name on it such as Palestine or Berlin or Moscow. Meanwhile, both players utter the names of the places they have landed on as a series of musical grunts. The singers can improvise, making their sounds as they chose, using the soundtrack as both backdrop and counterpoint. This activity should continue until the end of this intermezzo.)*

SCHOLEM

His ambition
was to write
a hundred lines
onto a single page
of ordinary note paper

So in August 1927,
he dragged me
to the Musée de Cluny
to show me
with true rapture
two grains of wheat
on which a kindred soul
inscribed the complete
Shema Yisroel

Shema Yisroel

The Complete Shema

**Shema**

**She-ma**

**Ma y'i**
**My**
**Mi**
**Zi**
**Mizi**
**My zi**
**My zion**

**Zion**

**Zion**

**Not yet Zion**

**Not yet**

*(Stage goes dark.)*

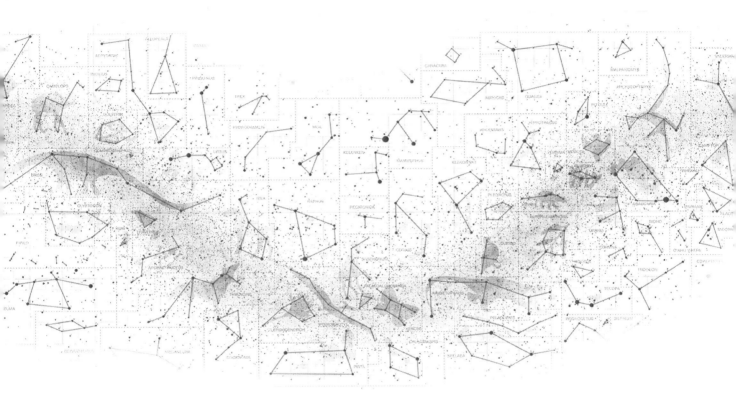

# SCENE III

## Svendborg 1934: The Brecht Time.

NARRATORS: *Dramaturgy. Anti-Socratic dialogues make sense in pastorals, sounds muffled in deep woods or fading over expanses of water. The treed paradise is the platform for nonsense, for the discredited meditative man. The book brought from elsewhere is now an anchor as is any voice that can be conjured. Vulnerable memory. But nonsense always floats upward, while the suicided personality, lost to social elements or weighed down by rhetoric, sinks to the bottom.*

| ON STAGE | PRE-RECORDED IMAGES & TEXT FOR MUSIC AND VIDEO |
|---|---|
| *(Lounge chairs on either side of the wall. Countryside, pines, bird sounds. Stage shades toward dark at rear where there are three low podiums on which lecturns are stationed. Benjamin enters from the right; Brecht from the left. They each sit down on the chairs downstage. Brecht is holding a copy of Dante. Scholem stands at lectern behind Benjamin.* | *(VIDEO: Svendborg. Nazis in power. Exile. Marxism vs. Fascism. Emigrating Jews, intellectuals.)* |

*Asja and Dora are at lecterns behind Brecht.*
*The singers at the lecterns are upstage and do*
*not interact with the characters downstage.)*

BRECHT

One thing I like
about Dante,
he can be read
out of doors.

BENJAMIN

While the sun
shines here,
all are in hell.

BRECHT
*(Looks around, pauses.)*

Truly wonderful machinery,
but of no use to us now.

BENJAMIN

Goodness in nature
goodness in man,
how they thought
in old Weimar.

It is a metaphysical truth,
all nature would lament

*(Various voices--but each word or phrase to be*
*only one sustained note.)*

**the fog**

**envelops**

**the road**

**the poplars**

58

if it were endowed
with words to speak.

BRECHT

What didn't they disguise
as reality?  Now we must
intervene on behalf
of ourselves.

That sham of the old state failed.
The proletariat employ us.

BENJAMIN

You read your Dante
in perfect light.

BRECHT

The old machinery . . .

BENJAMIN

The attainment of
technical progress
in literature
eventually changes
the function of the art form.

**the farms**

**and the artillery**

**and the artillery**

**envelops**

BRECHT

And the change
in the art form
affects the social order.

BENJAMIN

**the farms**

Thus it was in Moscow,
thus it will be.

Cities transformed
into utopian cells.
Love and progress
unrecognizable.

**the poplars**

(*Scholem, Asja and Dora sing facing the
audience.  They exaggerate the gesture of their
singing.*)

**the road**

SCHOLEM
(*writing a letter at the podium.*)

I gather things are bad.
I have just returned
from Tiberias,
desert gleaming
people-less,
to find your letter
on my desk.

**and the fog**

BENJAMIN

The current atmosphere!

In Russia, all are weary.
In Berlin, one looks first
at the little badges
on people's lapels,
then no longer wishes
to look them in the face.

BRECHT

You saw Asja?

BENJAMIN

Unrecognizable.

BRECHT

Asja, you saw?

BENJAMIN

Like an ice-melting fire.
But far away,
not the faintest
heat upon my face.

She was cold to me
—not indifferent,

**and the fog**

**envelops**

**the road**

**the poplars**

**the farms**

but active, as though
my wanting her
demanded
a political response.

                    BRECHT

Did it harden you
against the cause?

                    BENJAMIN

I often imagine
her time with me
as though I were being
investigated by a tribunal.

                    BRECHT

The enemy which drives
you from your books
will not be worn down
by the likes of us.

                    SCHOLEM

Have you studied Hebrew?
Those sounds
will soon be lost.

**and the artillery**

**and the artillery**

**envelops**

**the farms**

**the poplars**

BENJAMIN

Whoever wants to make
the hard thing give way
should miss no opportunity
for friendliness.

ASJA

In Europe,
we still have hope.

BRECHT

Tactics of attrition
are what you enjoy,
sitting under these
very pear trees in the shade.

As you turn everything
into a word, you falsify
its power.  As you turn
to the word, you
drop the gesture,
the hand which gestures
and which can hold a gun.

DORA

Never to Palestine,
say his friends.

**the road**

**and the fog**

**and the fog**

BENJAMIN

I lost no opportunity,
but even in her illness
she spurned our meetings
in order to attend re-education
sessions of bourgeois kulaks
who decried their wrongs
and rent their clothes
as though pulling down
the draperies
in their mansions.

Poor Meyerhold,
he too withered
beneath her glance.

SCHOLEM

You missed the Marseilles
boat for Jaffa.

ASJA

You fled Moscow
before the thaw.

BRECHT

Meyerhold?
What news do you have
of the man?

**envelops**

**the road**

**the poplars**

**the farms**

BENJAMIN

Asja's and Reich's critiques
were fodder for the censors.
The Central Committee
had him under review.

The critics are commissars.
The writers search
for the rule of their
necessity.

Therefore,
the true measure
of life is memory.

Meyerhold
followed his own way.
The party hacks
put his plays
through the meat-grinders
of their theories.

BRECHT

Yes, it is easy
to find ideological
flaws in Meyerhold's
productions, even
if they are not there.

But you discussed this
with Asja?

**and the artillery**

**and the artillery**

**envelops**

65

BENJAMIN

She was very harsh,
mixing my defense
of him with her
unease with me.

So again
the Revolution
swallows up
its children.

BRECHT

You complain too much.
Your mother was
bourgeois Berlin.
You only know the hunger
that you choose.

ASJA

Love and lamentation
belong to the past.

BRECHT

One who fights for the exploited
is exiled from love
as well as country.

Tomorrow will bring

the farms

the poplars

the road

and the fog

such disasters
your love life
will seem of
no significance.

BENJAMIN

I showed myself
not clever enough
for this world,
when to be clever
would have done
a lot for me.

Especially with Asja.

BRECHT

I was her teacher,
before you met her.

Not only theater.                    **and the fog**
Not only politics.
I taught her how
to wash herself.

Before, she used                     **envelops**
to wash only
not to be dirty.

But, as far as I                     **the road**
was concerned,

*that* was insufficient,
absolutely
out of the question.

So I showed her
how she must scrub
her face, how to give
herself time and patience.

After awhile, she
became perfect at it,
and I wanted nothing more
than to film her as she washed.

                BENJAMIN

You saw her politically,
a creature you could correct.

                BRECHT

It's true, we were never lovers.

                BENJAMIN

O bourgeois heart!

I followed her,
a doomed aristocrat
rolling in a tumbrel
to where the axe must fall.

**the poplars**

**the farms**

**and the artillery**

BRECHT

Accept your exile.

DORA

Neither Hebrew nor Russian
could he learn.

BENJAMIN
(*To himself.*)

This is no time
for lamentations.

Lamentations
are of the past.

This is no time
for more
than fleeting touch
in the new streets
of our soul.

In Moscow, she hid
her body from me.

She never let me see
her wash her face.

**and the artillery**

**envelops**

**the farms**

ASJA

You fled Moscow
before the work
was finished.

You fled
before the thaw
would bring us
back to life.

You left while ice
hid paving stones,
made all our
walking treacherous.

BRECHT

It's plain to me
why people don't
examine the injuries
of others more closely.

They are convinced
of the pain
because it is they
who have inflicted it.

BENJAMIN

More difficult
to see is the hurt

inflicted on oneself.
The violence of the spirit
meets actuality.

There is nothing so whole
as a cleft heart.

*(Scholem, Asja and Dora make slight gutteral
sounds, collect their papers from the lecterns
and walk off stage.  Stage goes dark.)*

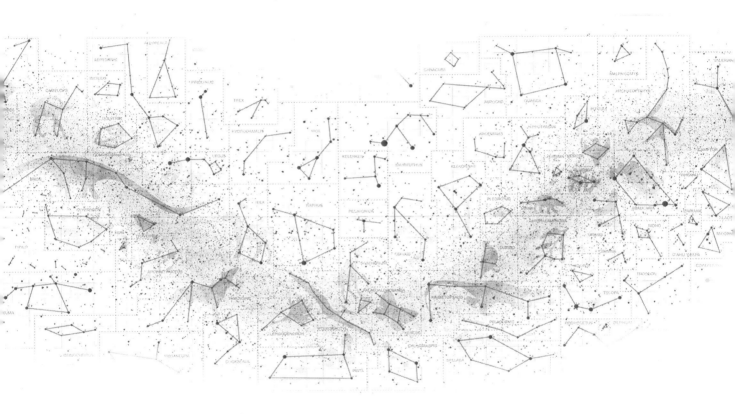

# Intermezzo: Letter Exchange

| ON STAGE | PRE-RECORDED IMAGES & TEXT FOR MUSIC AND VIDEO |
|---|---|

*(Benjamin is at his desk in Berlin. Scholem is at his desk in Jerusalem. When they sing, there should be some suggestion that they are singing over the wall at each other.)*

### BENJAMIN

I moved in clouds of dust
and under a mountain of books.

### SCHOLEM

Not to Palestine, but
to another of Berlin's
forbidding streets.

*(Duo.)*

**In the *enfer* of the library
where erotica is kept.**

### BENJAMIN

I unpacked my books.
And lovingly
wiped them clean
with an old rag.

SCHOLEM

You await marching
in the street, boot
stamped over the page,
blood of frenzied thought.

BENJAMIN

Messiah and geography
never coincide.

SCHOLEM

First things:
unriddle kabbalah,
unriddle texts

BENJAMIN

First things,
reading how despair
inscribes itself
in the city's text.

(*Stage goes dark.*)

**In the *enfer* of the library,
word and dream are met.**

**Impotency and longing,
text against flesh.**

**O silence as weeping.**

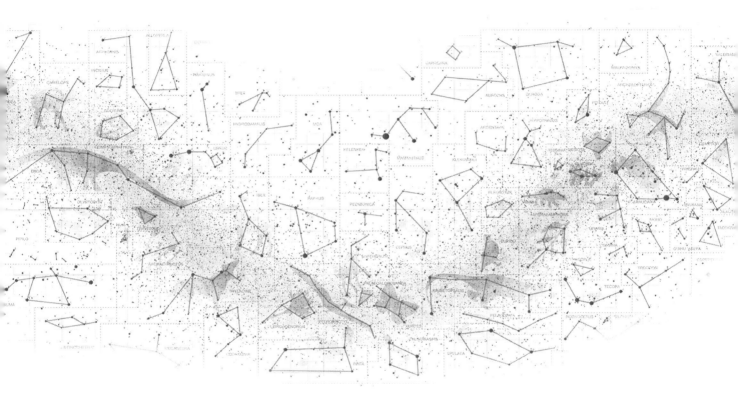

# SCENE IV

## Paris 1939: In The Arcades.

NARRATORS: *Apogee of thought. Style will protect the truth in oneself. Gesture reaching out to embrace contingency. The flaneur is aswim in boulevard crowds: first he takes the short chop strokes of the crawl, then he performs the butterfly, arms circling, parting the sea of people. Finally in despair, he dives beneath their bobbing heads. Where are the crowd's feet planted, where do the urban masses root down, what substance do they stand on in the Tuileries, on the paving stones before Metro Opera or Madeleine, in the passage ways of the 1st or the 2nd? Nothing of my own.*

| ON STAGE | PRE-RECORDED IMAGES & TEXT FOR MUSIC AND VIDEO |
|---|---|
| *(Lights up. Benjamin is standing, faces forward.)* | *(VIDEO: Paris. Research in the Bibliothèque, research on the boulevards and arcades. Baudelaire, flaneurs. Siren voices in Palestine and New York. Germany in full mobilization.)* |

79

CHORUS

**In the windswept stairwells
of the Eiffel Tower,
in the steel supports
of the bridge,
hopes flow through
nets of iron.**

**Tunnels of merchandising
in the blocks of flats.**

**Industrial luxury
and its effects.**

**The arcades are
a Babel of desires
making a few men rich.**

BENJAMIN

From what ruins
to excavate a life?

Can one walk in a city
and not give heart
to utter loneliness?

This debris is sacred,
broken stones
are modifications
of broken eons.

Now they talk to me,
whispering in lieu
of love's absence:
*I am the home of all dreams.*


SCHOLEM
(*Enters from left, faces forward.*)

Your tongue is doubled,
materialist and mystic,
and you wander in Gehenna.

Ultimately, you must sue
for your own singularity.

BENJAMIN

Progress leans
its fine elbows
on the new.

No need to dream!

All that happens
rises to another plane,
neither divine nor profane,
but gleaming with
the power of
a commodity.

**Chased from Germany
did you not seek
a new language
as Moses needed Aaron
for his speech?**

Streetwalkers
supply all else.

SCHOLEM

Here in New York,
at the Institute,
they are convinced
that, in dealing with you,
they are dealing with
a mystic.

BENJAMIN

So much lies in the way
of childhood's memories.

Unplanned Paris,
its spiraled streets worming
as if toward hope.

Ghostly processions.
Profane motifs.

Baudelaire dragging
his shadow
like a foul black wing.

SCHOLEM

They accuse you
of mental alchemy.

**"Meryon: the sea of buildings,
the ruins, the clouds,
the majesty and decrepitude
of Paris."**

**Windswept stairwells,
Eiffel Tower,
steel supports,
the bridge,
nets of iron.**

**merchandising
blocks of flats.**

## BENJAMIN

What makes even
the new into a ruin?

All those
who could not speak,
whose hopes
were locked away:

Their words
proclaim their longing
for what in their name
was never done.

So I kept
to the broken tongue
of desiring,
which like a city
speaks thousands
of dialects.

## SCHOLEM

It stands to reason,
the obvious victim
is your Hebrew studies.

Ancient times and now
clash blasphemously
in your soul.

**luxury
and its effects.**

**babels of desires
a few rich men.**

**Chased from Germany
did you not seek
a new language
as Moses needed Aaron
for his speech?**

BENJAMIN

Shops enunciate
the great poem
of display.

They hide wishes
as though each thing
marched in a parade
of ghosts.

*Ur*-history of the present!

Goods cram shelves,
cloth lies in the drapers'
battings, and perfumes
scent the roiled air—

Impermissibly poetic!

Higher forces
driving me from
my most mystical sources.

ADORNO
(*Enters from right, faces forward.*)

In its present form,
we cannot entertain
the publication
of this writing.

(*Trio.*)

**They sleep.**
**The divine word**
**strikes them.**

**And they dream.**
**Who has excavated**
**the dream?**

BENJAMIN

(*Goes to writing desk.*)

My Dear Brecht,

The letter you
addressed to me
from Denmark
at long last
found its way to Paris.

I have fallen
into the hands
of the genuine
magicians

who when lost
in meditations
practice numerology
in the casinos.

Otherwise,
I'm with tourists
who reward me
with nothing.

SCHOLEM

And I write you too,
wanting you to know
that here in Tiberius—

BENJAMIN

*Tiberius,* the name
hooks all that is archaic,
a film of sweet wine
left on the tongue.

Time has created a hallowed
place for it, cupped it
in dead and ancient myth.

I am foresworn from this.

(*Puts aside letter to Brecht and starts new one.*)

Dear Gerhard,

Books and reflections,
and all the time
to myself, since most
of my acquaintances
think themselves
too cultured
to play cards.

Recently, I
entertained myself
making a list
of mistakes and failures
over the last two years.

Misery and exuberance

are thus synthesized
in my researches.

(*Puts Scholem letter aside and goes back to the*
*one to Brecht.*)

Berthold, I showed
myself not clever
enough for this world.

See, now, it is only
in the actual
of things that there
is reason not to lose
courage in the struggle
for existence.

(*Blackout. Lights come on.*
*Top of wall is level with floor and Adorno,*
*Scholem and Benjamin are assembled on*
*stage.*)

ADORNO

My dear colleague,
you construe,

you construe
the oldest
with the new

and the archaic

becomes an addition
to the newest
instead of being
just the newest!

BENJAMIN

He construes,
he construes

that the oldest
is the newest,

that the myth
has been backdated

instead of being
truly seen
as a phantasmagoria
from the depths of hell.

ADORNO and BENJAMIN

We construe, we construe
and Kafka comes in too!

The commodity
survives to no purpose.

SCHOLEM

They construe, they construe.

But they should weave
some lifelines too.

The jackbooted wolf
is everywhere.

(*Blackout.  Lights come on and Benjamin is at
his desk, letter in hand.*)

BENJAMIN

We bourgeois characters
lack the height
from which to fall
into the depths.

And now, subvention
from the Institute
is at an end, my
sole means of subsistence.

All sorts of life,
flashing dreams,
possess my being.
But the charms
exerted on me
by the world
are too weak,
the prizes
of posterity
too uncertain.

Suicide often seems
a reasonable
alternative
to literature.

Asja in my dreams.
Dora who saved me from myself.
Baudelaire hovers.

(*Stage dims.*)

BRECHT
(*Standing in shadows.*)

Stalin's trials?

BENJAMIN

Finished in 1939
with Russia for good.

SCHOLEM

I despair of you
making this journey,
and besides the times
are not good.

BENJAMIN

Strange hope in Europe

wearing a death's head.

ASJA
(*She is standing in shadows.*)

They are at the door
to swallow me into the night.
O Russia!

BENJAMIN

So long ago,
when the Great War began
when Heinle and his lover
took their lives . . .

BELMORE
(*Voice from offstage.*)

My, you are in a state.

91

# Intermezzo: Voices In Near Darkness

| ON STAGE | PRE-RECORDED IMAGES & TEXT FOR MUSIC AND VIDEO |
|---|---|

*(Stage is near dark, voices muted.)*

SCHOLEM

The appearance of *Torah*
is the result of the knowledge
of good and evil.

BENJAMIN

All visible law
is law-making violence.

Only the violence of God
or the general strike
can counter the violence
of the bloody law.

SCHOLEM

God?  A general strike?

As usual, Walter, you seem
somewhere in the middle,
or should I say muddle?

BENJAMIN

I walk not knowing
whether my heart is full
or whether my soul is full.

I would like to keep silent.

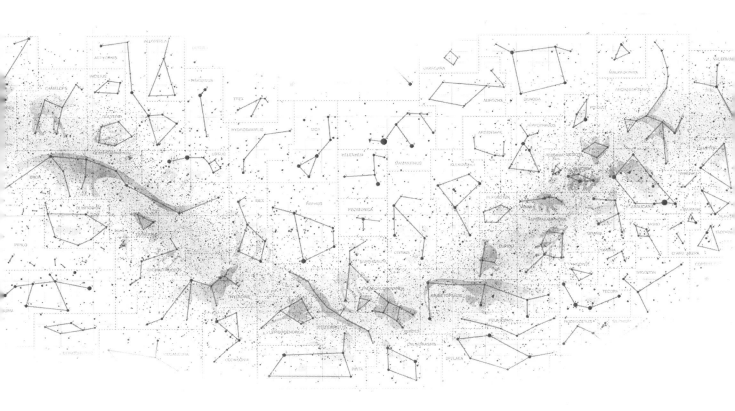

# SCENE V

## Paris, Stade Colombe, Nevers 1939-1940:
## Internment and Non-internment.

NARRATORS: *Nothing of one's own. Least, still lost. Anachronism: target on one's back. The availability of victims is impressive. Sing a song of handmaidens, transports and media. Thesis Z on History: what can't be imagined will definitely happen.*

| ON STAGE | PRE-RECORDED IMAGES & TEXT FOR MUSIC AND VIDEO |
|---|---|
| *(Hints of a makeshift prison. BENJAMIN and SAHL on stage.)* | *(VIDEO: Occupation. Roundups. Martial displays. Refugees. Jackboots in the streets.)* |
| BENJAMIN | |
| There are still positions left to defend in Europe. And Paris seems the place. | |

97

SAHL

Are you mad?

All immigrants
from Germany and Austria
must report to the Stade Colombe.

To remain there until transport to internment
camps at Nevers is arranged.

BENJAMIN

Listen!  One hears pandemonium,
a thousand bees buzzing
against a screen.

Here the confusion
of languages triumphs.

The new is being prepared
though we are not to be redeemed
by our sufferings.

SAHL

I heard heavy vehicles rolling.

In the grey dawn
of the tenth day
we were assembled.

*(Sung in a plaintive style by a small ensemble.)*

***Agunah!***
**The deserted wife.**

***Agunah!***

Creatures deceptively wordy
and yet totally abandoned.

Who could find a Dante
to depict this scene?

### BENJAMIN

What clarity to look
into enormity, unbending
in my belief that,
in the darkest times,
truth must show its face.

### SAHL

Walter sat apart,
preternaturally silent
for a change—
somewhere between shock,
fatigue and a sense
that, at last, he had
come upon a revelation.

### BENJAMIN

A bus took us through
Paris streets, past
the cafes where I once sat
with Céline, Drieu la Rochelle
and the exquisite Cocteau.

**Abandoned by the husband
and by the lawgiving rabbis.**

*Agunah!*
**Knowing what it is
to be attached
and detached.**

We were quite busy then.

Junger was translating farewell letters
of hostages soon to be shot.

Carl Schmitt was reworking Baudelaire.

The Bibliothèque.
Daily it disgorged
its riches, made them
available to my
unceasing pen.

Alas, Jouhandeau's pamphlet,
*Le peril juif* was selling well.

                SAHL

How lovely the old station
draped in morning fog.

              BENJAMIN

Everywhere, despite incredible pain, re-
deeming images.

                SAHL

Sealed trains were lined up
for us at Gare D'Austerlitz.

BENJAMIN

At the center of this world,
despair and hope.

SAHL

Yet I sensed in the air
a foreclosure of sorts.

BENJAMIN

Already it is dark.
Do we sleep on the floor?

SAHL

I fear day will also
bring us darkness.

BENJAMIN

There are still things
to defend.  In the dawn
I will organize lectures
on Marx and Freud.

SAHL

Why talk of "proletarianization"
of the Jews?

*(Images of the camp.  The castle at Nevers, etc.*
*appear on video screen.)*

Already we are imprisoned
in hovels.

Yet, behind a dirty curtain,
Walter has organized
a literary magazine.

I have been commissioned
to write an essay about
our situation:
"The Emergence of a Society
From Nothingness."

Such activities
showed Benjamin's genius
for the impractical.

                    BENJAMIN

Demons bother me less
than the mute horror
of looking into an abyss.

Even this disaster
is shot through with
facets of the Messiah,
who comes only when all
is lost.

(*Lights out.  Then lights on. A Paris cafe.
Benjamin sits writing.*)

**At that time
"Auschwitz" was unknown to us.**

BENJAMIN

My dear Adorno    My existence
is dominated by utter uncertainty
as to what the next day or next hour
will bring to us.

The news of war, of
the occupation, is reduced
to a single summons.

I am to be the voice
of the messenger of misfortune.

To return to the question
of the visa . . .

To return to the question
of the visa.

(*Quick blackout, then lights come up.*)

BENJAMIN

My dear Professor Horkheimer,
It will surely be unnecessary
for me to repeat my request,
namely that you intervene
as quickly and expeditiously
with the American authorities.

(*Quick blackout, then lights come up.*)

*Agunah!*
**Truest knowing
unsupported by
authority.**

A letter from the consulate certifying that I can expect my visa with virtually no delay would be of primary importance to me.

(*Quick blackout, then lights come up. Benjamin sings his lines in alternation with the chorus on the video track.*)

Dear Gerhard,

The way things now stand,

the question of whether it

will be possible to assure me

sustenance in Palestine for

a number of months becomes

important. (I don't imagine

that this can be financed

from your own funds.)

As things stand,

among the various danger zones

SCHOLEM

**Horkheimer addresses
not a single sentence
to the topic he announces:
"The Jews and Europe."**

**The problem of the Jews' expulsion, the
meaning and significance, he does not see.**

**Nor does he ask on behalf of the Jews:**

**What would Europe look like
after the elimination of the Jews?**

(*Chorus.*)

**In the evening,**

**our dreadful evening,**

**we came to Port Bou,**

into which the earth

is divided for Jews,

currently, France is the most

dangerous for me . . .

(*Stage goes dark.*)

**at the police station**

**we requested our entry stamps,**

**our entry stamps.**

**We cried, we begged,**

**we despaired**

**for an hour.**

**We cried for an hour,**

**we begged for that hour,**

**we despaired.**

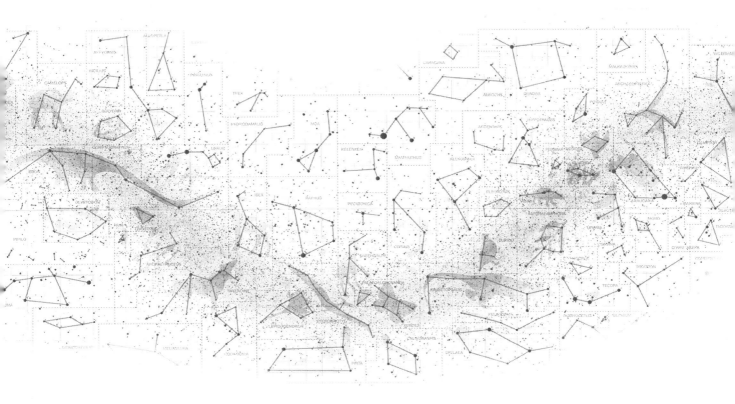

# EPILOGUE:

## Constellations Of Waking

NARRATORS:  *Benjamin is dead by his own hand.*

| ON STAGE | PRE-RECORDED IMAGES & TEXT FOR MUSIC AND VIDEO |
|---|---|
| (*All of the named characters except Benjamin are assembled to sing the epilogue.*) | |
| Something you wrote<br>"Eternity is far more<br>the rustle of a dress<br><br>than an idea."<br>What odd sounds<br>to listen to | |

beneath occluded skies
that darken rivers,
Dnieper, Havel, Ebro,

murmuring contained
between
their tree lined banks . . .

"In the fields
with which we are concerned,

knowledge comes only
in flashes.  The text
is thunder rolling

long afterwards."
And thus, and thus . . .

\*

These constellations,
which are not composed of stars
but the curls of shrivelled leaves

by which the tree expressed
the notion of the storm.  You
lived in storm, your outer life

"adversities on all sides
which sometimes came
as wolves."  Your father—

Europe was your father
who cast you on the path,
hungry, into constellated cities

Berlin, Moscow, Paris.
Where would
Minerva's owl alight,

on what dark branch
to display its polished
talons?

*

1940
and in Paris, the library
is lost.

Books
no longer on the shelves
how sweetly

they were "touched," you wrote
"by the mild boredom
of order."

*

Curled leaf,
one among many
on trees that lead

to a border crossing.
But black wolves in France,
they have changed the idea

of eternity.  Toward
Port Bou, bright dust
mixing

with the ocean's salt air.
Wave fleck from train,
each spun light

must have its meaning.
So to consider
as ultimate work

that sea bed of
all citation
you'd allow nothing of your own

thus the perfected volume.
No author?
And then no death?

The sea is inscribed
with *The Prayer
for the Dead.*  No

author and then
no death?  But the leaf
acquired shadow by

the ideal of light,
scattered light
the father

never recognizes.
The books are not
on shelves,

for that was Paris.
This the closed road
from Port Bou

which glistens with the dew
of morning.  Redemptive
time

which crystallizes
as tree, as leaf
on the way to a border.

CHORUS
(*Something hurdy-gurdian in the song of the
following.*)

**He climbed a labyrinth,
a labyrinth of stairs,
past other stairways
descending.**

113

He climbed
a labyrinth of stairs,
each step tested
with his foot.

Always tentative,
always hopeful,
while nearby,
other stairs descended.

Breathlessly
he rose,
up to their heights.
Chest aching,

thoughts twisting
between his temples,
head pounding
with his blood.

He felt lightheaded,
fearing always
each step
would carry him
into thinning air.

*(Stage goes dark.)*

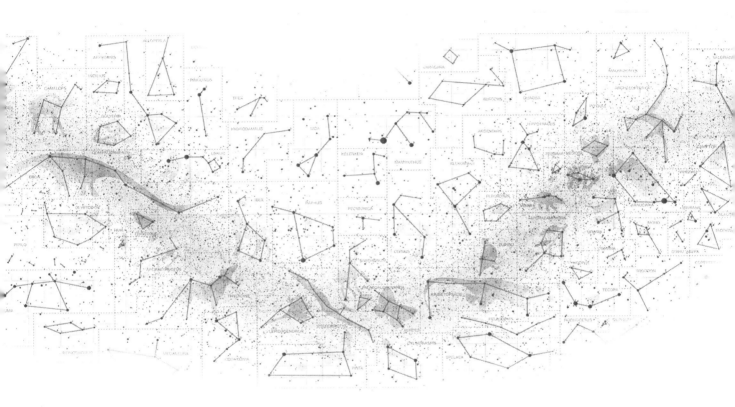

# NOTES ON CONCEPT AND PERFORMANCE

This work is concerned with the life and death of Walter Benjamin (1892-1940), one of the most important writers and thinkers of the modern era.  Benjamin's life constitutes, in a profound sense, a moral and intellectual tale of the fate of the creative individual enmeshed in the terrible history of the first half of the twentieth century. Benjamin was attracted to and participated uneasily in the major cultural and social movements of his time.  His involvements ranged from the idealistic youth movements of his early years through flirtations with Marxism, messianic Judaism and the intense literary and artistic battlegrounds of modernism in which he befriended such major thinkers and artists as Berthold Brecht, Gershom Scholem, Hugo von Hofmannsthal and Rilke.  Throughout, Benjamin sought for a "poetics" of history, one that would yield a redemptive view of the past as seeded with "chips of messianic time," as he called them, images in which "the past and the now flash into constellations," each a nexus of knowledge and power against social and political oppression.

In this work, prologue, scenes and epilogue incorporating music, text, singers, video-sound track and other media focus on central dramatic moments in Benjamin's life and death.  The scenes juxtapose action, interior speech, dialogue and confrontation between characters to produce structures of sound and image presenting the entanglements of Benjamin's life and thought, especially as related to the themes which preoccupied him throughout his life: fate, idealism, moral choice, personal and social salvation.  Intermezzi between scenes provide ironic commentary on the development in the scenes.

The dramatic tension of the work is created through the depiction of Benjamin's immersion in the catastrophic events of the century and the choices they forced upon him, up to and including his final decision to take his own life rather than fall into the hands of the Nazis. The video-sound track, which is used for scene-setting, commentary, occasional flash forward and back, is meant to function like a Greek chorus, providing both emphasis and counterpoint to the events on stage. The guiding intention behind the construction of the work is, in the spirit of its central character, Benjamin, to create a series of "constellations" which would both move and instruct the audience.

This idea of a constellation is meant to be carried over into the way the work is performed. A constellation is created or perceived by the imposition of a structure on a set of data or events (an array of stars, a series of brushstrokes or musical notes) which is not originally part of these discrete events. The constellation is, in effect, an interpretation of the data. Thus the interrelations between elements in this work, between its voices and between the words, the music and other aspects of the *mise en scène*, are to be realized as a series of expressive tensions, somewhat less part of an ongoing narrative than as constituting the elements of a complex situation which any particular scene is depicting. I have tried to indicate, through the words, the implicit hope and dread that are the force-lines between the concrete elements. Thus, characters, even when they are singing in dialogue with each other, should also show forth a certain awareness of isolation but also of being caught in a matrix of time, history and place that shapes their language and the tone in which they deliver that language. My prefatory narrations to each scene (which should be declaimed) are meant to suggest the possible tonalities as well as the dictates of language under historical pressures. Likewise, the other elements of the work ought to emphasize that admixture of similitude and difference which make up a constellation.

A performer using a phantasmagoria (a kind of magic lantern) throwing image after image on to the stage would enhance the illusionistic aspect of the work. After all, what is more illusionistic than a constellation?

# SOURCES

Benjamin, Walter. *The Arcades Project.* Translated by Howard Eiland and Kevin McLaughlin. Prepared on the basis of the German volume edited by Rolf Tiedemann. Cambridge: The Belknap Press of Harvard University Press, 1999.

_____. *Illuminations.* Edited and with an Introduction by Hannah Arendt. Translated by Harry Zohn. New York: Schocken, 1969.

_____. *Reflections: Essays, Aphorisms, Autobiographical Writings.* Edited and with an Introduction by Peter Demetz. New York: Schocken, 1978.

_____. *Selected Writings: volume 1, 1913-1926.* Edited by Marcus Bullock and Michael W. Jennings. Cambridge: The Belknap Press of Harvard University, 1996.

_____. *Selected Writings: volume 2, 1927-1934.* Edited by Marcus Bullock and Michael W. Jennings. Cambridge: The Belknap Press of Harvard University, 1999.

_____. *Selected Writings: volume 3, 1935-1938.* Edited by Marcus Bullock and Michael W. Jennings. Cambridge: The Belknap Press of Harvard University, 2002.

_____. *Selected Writings: volume 4, 1938-1940.* Edited by Marcus Bullock and Michael W. Jennings. Cambridge: The Belknap Press of Harvard University, 2003.

_____. *The Correspondence of Walter Benjamin: 1910-1940*. Edited and Annotated by Gershom Scholem and Theodor W. Adorno. Translated by Manfred R. Jacobson and Evelyn M. Jacobson. Chicago and London: The University of Chicago Press, 1994.

_____. *The Correspondence of Walter Benjamin and Gershom Scholem: 1932-1940*. Edited by Gershom Scholem. Translated by Gary Smith and Andre Lefevere. Introduction by Anson Rabinbach. Cambridge: Harvard University Press, 1992.

_____. *Understanding Brecht.* Introduction by Stanley Mitchell. London: New Left Books, 1973.

Brecht, Berthold. *Poems 1913-1956.* New York: Theatre Art Books, 1997.

Handelman, Susan. *Fragments of Redemption: Jewish Thought & Literary Theory in Benjamin, Scholem & Levinas.* Bloomington: Indiana University Press, 1991.

Heller, Michael. *In The Builded Place.* Minneapolis: Coffee House Press, 1989.

Johnson, Ellen Fishman. Excerpts from *Constellations of Waking.* https://soundcloud.com/efjcomposer/sets/benjamin-a-multimedia-opera
_____Website: http://www.efjcomposer.com/

Scholem, Gershom. *Gershom Scholem: A Life in Letters, 1914-1982.* Edited and Translated by Anthony David Skinner. Cambridge: Harvard University Press, 2002.

Sontag, Susan. *Under the Sign of Saturn.* New York: Farrar, Straus and Giroux, 1980.

# ILLUSTRATIONS

Photo, page xxix: Maquette of stage for *Constellations of Waking* designed by the sculptor, Bradford Graves, 1999.

Photo, page 3: Walter Benjamin's membership card for the Bibliothèque nationale de France (1940).

Photo, page 7: Slip-in card for stereopticon, Potsdamer Platz II, Berlin.

Photo, page 33:  Moscow winter street scene, *1926.*

Photo, page 57: Berthold Brecht and Walter Benjamin, 1934, Skovsbostrand, Denmark, Photographer unknown.

Photo, page 79: Passage des Panoramas, Paris, @ 1900.

Photo, page 97: Registering for internment, Paris, 1939, photographer unknown.

Photo, page 109: panel of *Passengen-Hommage à Walter Benjamin* by Dani Karavan, at Port Bou, photographed by the author.  (See Acknowledgments, p *iii*)

# ABOUT THE AUTHOR

MICHAEL HELLER's poems first appeared in print in the nine-teen-sixties while he was living in a small village on Spain's Andalu-sian coast, a period he describes in his book, *Earth and Cave* (Dos Madres Press, 2006). In 1967, he returned to the U.S, taking a teaching position at New York University. Since then, he has pub-lished over twenty-five volumes of poetry, essays, memoir and fiction. Among his most recent works are *Speaking the Estranged: Essays on the Work of George Oppen* (2012), *This Constellation Is A Name: Collected Poems 1965-2010* (2012) and *Dianoia* (2016). Since the nineteen-nineties, he has been collaborating with the composer El-len Fishman Johnson on multimedia works including writing the li-bretto published here for the opera, *Constellations of Waking*, which premiered at the Philadelphia Fringe Festival in 2000. Among his many awards are grants and prizes from the National Endowment for the Humanities, the New York Foundation for the Arts, the Po-etry Society of America and The Fund for Poetry. A collection of critical essays on his work, *The Poetry and Poetics of Michael Heller: A Nomad Memory* was published by Fairleigh Dickinson University Press in 2015. A frequent traveler to Europe, he resides in New York City and spends his summers in the Colorado mountains. He is married to the poet and scholar Jane Augustine.

Other books by Michael Heller
published by Dos Madres Press

A Look at the Door with the Hinges Off (2006)
Earth and Cave (2007)


He is also included in:
Realms of the Mothers:
The First Decade of Dos Madres Press - 2016

For the full Dos Madres Press catalog:
www.dosmadres.com